50 Mediterranean Flavors for Every Meal

By: Kelly Johnson

Table of Contents

- Greek Lemon Chicken Soup
- Mediterranean Quinoa Salad
- Hummus with Roasted Red Peppers
- Spanakopita (Spinach Pie)
- Tabbouleh Salad
- Shakshuka (Poached Eggs in Tomato Sauce)
- Fattoush Salad
- Baba Ganoush
- Moroccan Lamb Tagine
- Grilled Halloumi with Vegetables
- Falafel with Tahini Sauce
- Grilled Sardines with Lemon and Herbs
- Moussaka
- Caprese Salad
- Chicken Souvlaki
- Couscous with Vegetables and Chickpeas
- Grilled Octopus with Olive Oil and Lemon
- Cretan Dakos (Barley Rusk Salad)
- Greek Yogurt with Honey and Nuts
- Pasta Puttanesca
- Lentil Soup with Spinach and Lemon
- Baklava
- Stuffed Grape Leaves
- Mediterranean Tuna Salad
- Roasted Eggplant with Tahini Sauce
- Seafood Paella
- Greek-Style Roast Lamb
- Fennel and Orange Salad
- Ratatouille
- Grilled Eggplant with Feta Cheese
- Lemon and Herb Roasted Potatoes
- Octopus Salad
- Mediterranean Chicken with Olives and Capers
- Tzatziki Sauce
- Spinach and Feta Stuffed Chicken Breast

- Orzo Salad with Tomatoes and Feta
- Mediterranean Shrimp Scampi
- Zaatar Roasted Chicken
- Saganaki (Fried Cheese)
- Greek Meatballs with Yogurt Sauce
- Lemon and Garlic Marinated Olives
- Mediterranean Veggie Pita Wraps
- Grilled Zucchini with Mint and Garlic
- Chickpea Stew with Spinach and Tomatoes
- Roasted Red Pepper and Feta Dip
- Grilled Lamb Chops with Garlic and Rosemary
- Couscous-Stuffed Bell Peppers
- Greek-Style Braised Okra
- Lemon and Herb Grilled Sea Bass
- Pita Bread with Olive Oil and Herbs

Greek Lemon Chicken Soup (Avgolemono)

Ingredients:

- 1 cup cooked chicken, shredded
- 6 cups chicken broth
- 1/3 cup long-grain rice or orzo
- 3 large eggs
- 1/4 cup fresh lemon juice (about 1-2 lemons)
- Salt and pepper to taste
- Fresh parsley or dill, chopped (optional, for garnish)

Instructions:

1. **Cook the Rice or Orzo**: In a large pot, bring the chicken broth to a boil. Add the rice or orzo and cook until tender, about 10-12 minutes.
2. **Prepare the Chicken**: Add the shredded chicken to the pot and reduce the heat to low, allowing it to warm through.
3. **Make the Avgolemono Sauce**:
    - In a medium bowl, beat the eggs until frothy.
    - Gradually whisk in the lemon juice.
    - Slowly add a ladleful of the hot chicken broth into the egg and lemon mixture, whisking continuously to temper the eggs and prevent curdling.
    - Repeat with another ladleful of broth.
4. **Combine and Serve**:
    - Slowly pour the egg mixture back into the soup pot, stirring continuously until the soup thickens slightly. Do not let it boil.
    - Season with salt and pepper to taste.
    - Remove from heat and serve hot, garnished with fresh parsley or dill if desired.

Mediterranean Quinoa Salad

Ingredients:

- 1 cup quinoa
- 2 cups water
- 1 cup cherry tomatoes, halved
- 1 cucumber, diced
- 1/2 red onion, finely chopped
- 1/4 cup Kalamata olives, pitted and sliced
- 1/4 cup feta cheese, crumbled
- 2 tbsp fresh parsley, chopped
- 2 tbsp fresh mint, chopped (optional)
- 1/4 cup extra virgin olive oil
- 2 tbsp lemon juice
- 1 tsp dried oregano
- Salt and pepper to taste

Instructions:

1. Rinse quinoa under cold water. In a medium saucepan, bring water to a boil. Add quinoa, reduce heat to low, cover, and simmer for 15 minutes or until water is absorbed. Fluff with a fork and let it cool.
2. In a large bowl, combine quinoa, cherry tomatoes, cucumber, red onion, olives, feta cheese, parsley, and mint.
3. In a small bowl, whisk together olive oil, lemon juice, oregano, salt, and pepper. Pour the dressing over the salad and toss to combine.
4. Serve immediately or refrigerate for later.

Hummus with Roasted Red Peppers

Ingredients:

- 1 can (15 oz) chickpeas, drained and rinsed
- 1 large red bell pepper, roasted, peeled, and seeds removed
- 1/4 cup tahini
- 2 tbsp olive oil
- 2 tbsp lemon juice
- 1 clove garlic, minced
- 1/2 tsp ground cumin
- Salt to taste
- Paprika and olive oil for garnish

Instructions:

1. In a food processor, combine chickpeas, roasted red pepper, tahini, olive oil, lemon juice, garlic, cumin, and salt. Blend until smooth and creamy.
2. Adjust seasoning to taste.
3. Transfer to a serving bowl, drizzle with olive oil, and sprinkle with paprika. Serve with pita bread or fresh vegetables.

Spanakopita (Spinach Pie)

Ingredients:

- 1 package (16 oz) frozen spinach, thawed and drained
- 1 cup feta cheese, crumbled
- 1/2 cup ricotta cheese
- 1/4 cup grated Parmesan cheese
- 1/2 cup fresh dill, chopped
- 1/2 cup green onions, chopped
- 2 cloves garlic, minced
- 2 eggs, beaten
- 1/2 tsp nutmeg
- Salt and pepper to taste
- 1 package (16 oz) phyllo dough, thawed
- 1/2 cup butter, melted

Instructions:

1. Preheat oven to 350°F (175°C).
2. In a large bowl, mix spinach, feta, ricotta, Parmesan, dill, green onions, garlic, eggs, nutmeg, salt, and pepper.
3. Lightly brush a 9x13-inch baking dish with butter. Layer half of the phyllo sheets, brushing each with butter.
4. Spread the spinach mixture evenly over the phyllo. Layer the remaining phyllo sheets on top, brushing each with butter.
5. Bake for 45-50 minutes or until golden brown. Let cool slightly before cutting into squares.

Tabbouleh Salad

Ingredients:

- 1/2 cup bulgur wheat
- 1 cup boiling water
- 1 large bunch parsley, finely chopped
- 1/4 cup fresh mint, finely chopped
- 2 tomatoes, diced
- 1 cucumber, diced
- 1/4 cup green onions, finely chopped
- 1/4 cup lemon juice
- 1/4 cup olive oil
- Salt and pepper to taste

Instructions:

1. Place bulgur in a bowl and pour boiling water over it. Cover and let sit for 15 minutes or until softened. Drain any excess water.
2. In a large bowl, combine bulgur, parsley, mint, tomatoes, cucumber, and green onions.
3. In a small bowl, whisk together lemon juice, olive oil, salt, and pepper. Pour over the salad and toss to combine.
4. Serve chilled or at room temperature.

Shakshuka (Poached Eggs in Tomato Sauce)

Ingredients:

- 2 tbsp olive oil
- 1 onion, chopped
- 1 red bell pepper, chopped
- 3 cloves garlic, minced
- 1 tsp ground cumin
- 1 tsp smoked paprika
- 1/4 tsp cayenne pepper (optional)
- 1 can (28 oz) crushed tomatoes
- Salt and pepper to taste
- 6 eggs
- Fresh cilantro or parsley for garnish

Instructions:

1. Heat olive oil in a large skillet over medium heat. Add onion and bell pepper, and sauté until softened.
2. Stir in garlic, cumin, paprika, and cayenne pepper. Cook for 1 minute.
3. Add crushed tomatoes, salt, and pepper. Simmer for 10-15 minutes until thickened.
4. Make small wells in the sauce and crack an egg into each well. Cover and cook until eggs are set.
5. Garnish with cilantro or parsley and serve with crusty bread.

Fattoush Salad

Ingredients:

- 2 pita breads, toasted and broken into pieces
- 2 tomatoes, diced
- 1 cucumber, diced
- 1/4 cup radishes, sliced
- 1/4 cup green onions, chopped
- 1/4 cup parsley, chopped
- 2 tbsp fresh mint, chopped
- 1/4 cup lemon juice
- 1/4 cup olive oil
- 1 tsp ground sumac
- Salt and pepper to taste

Instructions:

1. In a large bowl, combine pita bread pieces, tomatoes, cucumber, radishes, green onions, parsley, and mint.
2. In a small bowl, whisk together lemon juice, olive oil, sumac, salt, and pepper. Pour over the salad and toss to combine.
3. Serve immediately.

Baba Ganoush

Ingredients:

- 1 large eggplant
- 1/4 cup tahini
- 2 tbsp lemon juice
- 2 tbsp olive oil
- 2 cloves garlic, minced
- 1/2 tsp ground cumin
- Salt to taste
- Paprika and olive oil for garnish

Instructions:

1. Preheat oven to 400°F (200°C). Prick the eggplant with a fork and roast until soft, about 30-40 minutes. Let it cool, then peel and mash.
2. In a food processor, combine eggplant, tahini, lemon juice, olive oil, garlic, cumin, and salt. Blend until smooth.
3. Transfer to a serving bowl, drizzle with olive oil, and sprinkle with paprika. Serve with pita bread or vegetables.

Moroccan Lamb Tagine

Ingredients:

- 2 tbsp olive oil
- 1 large onion, chopped
- 3 cloves garlic, minced
- 1 tbsp ground cumin
- 1 tbsp ground cinnamon
- 1 tsp ground turmeric
- 1/2 tsp ground ginger
- 2 lbs lamb shoulder, cut into cubes
- 1 can (14 oz) diced tomatoes
- 1/2 cup dried apricots, chopped
- 1/4 cup almonds, toasted
- 1/4 cup fresh cilantro, chopped
- Salt and pepper to taste

Instructions:

1. Heat olive oil in a tagine or heavy pot over medium heat. Add onion and garlic, and sauté until softened.
2. Stir in spices and cook for 1 minute.
3. Add lamb and brown on all sides.
4. Stir in tomatoes, apricots, salt, and pepper. Cover and simmer for 1.5-2 hours until lamb is tender.
5. Garnish with almonds and cilantro before serving.

Grilled Halloumi with Vegetables

Ingredients:

- 1 block halloumi cheese, sliced
- 1 zucchini, sliced
- 1 bell pepper, sliced
- 1 red onion, sliced
- 2 tbsp olive oil
- 1 tsp dried oregano
- Salt and pepper to taste

Instructions:

1. Preheat grill to medium-high heat.
2. Toss vegetables with olive oil, oregano, salt, and pepper.
3. Grill vegetables until tender, about 5-7 minutes per side. Grill halloumi for 2-3 minutes per side until golden.
4. Serve halloumi with grilled vegetables.

Falafel with Tahini Sauce

Ingredients for Falafel:

- 1 1/2 cups dried chickpeas
- 1 large onion, chopped
- 4 cloves garlic, minced
- 1 cup fresh parsley, chopped
- 1/4 cup fresh cilantro, chopped
- 1 1/2 tsp ground cumin
- 1 1/2 tsp ground coriander
- 1/2 tsp ground cayenne pepper
- 1 1/2 tsp salt
- 1/2 tsp black pepper
- 1 tsp baking powder
- 4-6 tbsp flour (adjust as needed)
- Vegetable oil for frying

Ingredients for Tahini Sauce:

- 1/2 cup tahini
- 2 tbsp lemon juice
- 1 garlic clove, minced
- 2 tbsp water
- Salt to taste

Instructions:

1. Soak the chickpeas in plenty of water overnight. Drain and rinse before using.
2. In a food processor, pulse the soaked chickpeas, onion, garlic, parsley, cilantro, cumin, coriander, cayenne, salt, and pepper until well combined, but not pureed.
3. Add the baking powder and flour, and pulse to combine. If the mixture is too wet, add more flour, 1 tablespoon at a time, until it holds together.
4. Cover and refrigerate the mixture for at least 1 hour.
5. Form the mixture into small balls or patties.
6. Heat vegetable oil in a deep frying pan over medium heat. Fry the falafel in batches for 3-4 minutes until golden brown on all sides.
7. For the tahini sauce, whisk together tahini, lemon juice, garlic, water, and salt until smooth.
8. Serve the falafel with the tahini sauce and garnish with fresh herbs.

Grilled Sardines with Lemon and Herbs

Ingredients:

- 8-10 fresh sardines, cleaned and gutted
- 2 tbsp olive oil
- 1 lemon, sliced
- 2 tbsp fresh parsley, chopped
- 2 garlic cloves, minced
- Salt and pepper to taste

Instructions:

1. Preheat the grill to medium-high heat.
2. Rub the sardines with olive oil, salt, and pepper.
3. Place the sardines on the grill and cook for 3-4 minutes on each side, until the fish is tender and cooked through.
4. In a small bowl, mix the garlic, parsley, and lemon juice.
5. Once the sardines are cooked, drizzle the garlic-herb mixture over the fish.
6. Serve immediately with extra lemon wedges on the side.

Moussaka

Ingredients:

- 2 eggplants, sliced into 1/2-inch rounds
- 1 lb ground lamb or beef
- 1 onion, chopped
- 2 garlic cloves, minced
- 1 can (14.5 oz) diced tomatoes
- 1/4 cup red wine
- 1 tsp ground cinnamon
- 1/4 tsp ground nutmeg
- Salt and pepper to taste
- 1/4 cup fresh parsley, chopped
- 2 tbsp olive oil
- 1/4 cup butter
- 1/4 cup all-purpose flour
- 2 cups milk
- 1/2 cup grated Parmesan cheese
- 2 eggs, beaten

Instructions:

1. Preheat the oven to 375°F (190°C).
2. Slice the eggplants and season with salt. Place them on a baking sheet and roast for 20-25 minutes, until softened.
3. In a large pan, heat olive oil over medium heat. Add the ground meat, onion, and garlic, and cook until browned.
4. Add the tomatoes, red wine, cinnamon, nutmeg, salt, and pepper. Simmer for 15 minutes, until thickened.
5. In another pan, melt butter and whisk in the flour to make a roux. Gradually add the milk, whisking constantly until thickened. Stir in the Parmesan and beaten eggs to create the béchamel sauce.
6. In a baking dish, layer the eggplant slices, followed by the meat sauce, and then the béchamel sauce.
7. Repeat the layers, ending with a layer of béchamel.
8. Bake for 45 minutes until golden brown and bubbling. Let it rest for 10 minutes before serving.

Caprese Salad

Ingredients:

- 4 ripe tomatoes, sliced
- 1 lb fresh mozzarella cheese, sliced
- 1/4 cup fresh basil leaves
- 2 tbsp olive oil
- 1 tbsp balsamic vinegar
- Salt and pepper to taste

Instructions:

1. Arrange the tomato and mozzarella slices alternately on a platter.
2. Tuck fresh basil leaves between the slices.
3. Drizzle with olive oil and balsamic vinegar.
4. Season with salt and pepper.
5. Serve immediately as a refreshing appetizer or side dish.

Chicken Souvlaki

Ingredients:

- 2 lbs chicken breast, cut into cubes
- 1/4 cup olive oil
- 3 tbsp lemon juice
- 3 cloves garlic, minced
- 1 tbsp dried oregano
- 1 tsp ground cumin
- Salt and pepper to taste
- Wooden skewers, soaked in water

Instructions:

1. In a bowl, whisk together olive oil, lemon juice, garlic, oregano, cumin, salt, and pepper.
2. Add chicken cubes and marinate for at least 1 hour in the refrigerator.
3. Preheat grill to medium-high heat. Thread chicken onto skewers.
4. Grill for 8-10 minutes, turning occasionally, until cooked through.
5. Serve with pita bread and tzatziki sauce.

Couscous with Vegetables and Chickpeas

Ingredients:

- 1 cup couscous
- 1 cup boiling water
- 1 can (15 oz) chickpeas, drained and rinsed
- 1 zucchini, diced
- 1 bell pepper, diced
- 1 carrot, diced
- 2 tbsp olive oil
- 1 tsp ground cumin
- 1/2 tsp ground paprika
- Salt and pepper to taste
- Fresh parsley for garnish

Instructions:

1. Place couscous in a bowl and pour boiling water over it. Cover and let sit for 5 minutes, then fluff with a fork.
2. In a skillet, heat olive oil over medium heat. Add zucchini, bell pepper, and carrot, and sauté until tender.
3. Stir in chickpeas, cumin, paprika, salt, and pepper. Cook for 2-3 minutes.
4. Mix vegetables and chickpeas with couscous. Garnish with parsley and serve.

Grilled Octopus with Olive Oil and Lemon

Ingredients:

- 2 lbs octopus
- 1/4 cup olive oil
- 3 tbsp lemon juice
- 2 cloves garlic, minced
- 1 tsp dried oregano
- Salt and pepper to taste

Instructions:

1. Bring a large pot of water to a boil. Add octopus and simmer for 45 minutes or until tender. Drain and let cool.
2. Cut octopus into pieces and marinate with olive oil, lemon juice, garlic, oregano, salt, and pepper.
3. Preheat grill to medium-high heat. Grill octopus for 3-4 minutes per side until charred.
4. Serve immediately with extra lemon wedges.

Cretan Dakos (Barley Rusk Salad)

Ingredients:

- 4 barley rusks
- 2 large tomatoes, grated
- 1/4 cup crumbled feta cheese
- 1/4 cup Kalamata olives, pitted and sliced
- 2 tbsp capers
- 2 tbsp olive oil
- 1 tbsp red wine vinegar
- Salt and pepper to taste
- Fresh oregano for garnish

Instructions:

1. Soak barley rusks briefly in water to soften.
2. Place softened rusks on a serving plate. Top with grated tomatoes, feta cheese, olives, and capers.
3. Drizzle with olive oil and vinegar. Season with salt, pepper, and garnish with oregano.
4. Serve immediately.

Greek Yogurt with Honey and Nuts

Ingredients:

- 2 cups Greek yogurt
- 1/4 cup honey
- 1/4 cup walnuts or almonds, chopped

Instructions:

1. Divide Greek yogurt into serving bowls.
2. Drizzle honey over the yogurt.
3. Sprinkle with chopped nuts.
4. Serve as a dessert or breakfast.

Pasta Puttanesca

Ingredients:

- 12 oz pasta (spaghetti or penne)
- 2 tbsp olive oil
- 3 cloves garlic, minced
- 1 can (14.5 oz) diced tomatoes
- 1/2 cup Kalamata olives, pitted and chopped
- 2 tbsp capers, drained
- 1/4 tsp red pepper flakes
- 1 tbsp anchovy paste (optional)
- Salt and pepper to taste
- Fresh parsley, chopped for garnish

Instructions:

1. Cook pasta according to package instructions until al dente. Drain and set aside.
2. Heat olive oil in a large pan over medium heat. Add garlic and sauté for 1-2 minutes until fragrant.
3. Add the diced tomatoes, olives, capers, red pepper flakes, and anchovy paste (if using). Stir well and simmer for 10 minutes, allowing the flavors to meld together.
4. Toss the cooked pasta into the sauce and combine. Season with salt and pepper to taste.
5. Serve the pasta with fresh parsley as a garnish.

Lentil Soup with Spinach and Lemon

Ingredients:

- 1 cup dried lentils, rinsed
- 1 tbsp olive oil
- 1 onion, chopped
- 2 carrots, chopped
- 2 celery stalks, chopped
- 2 garlic cloves, minced
- 1 can (14.5 oz) diced tomatoes
- 4 cups vegetable broth
- 4 cups fresh spinach, chopped
- 1 lemon, juiced
- 1 tsp ground cumin
- Salt and pepper to taste

Instructions:

1. In a large pot, heat olive oil over medium heat. Add the onion, carrots, celery, and garlic. Cook for 5-7 minutes, until softened.
2. Add the lentils, tomatoes, vegetable broth, cumin, salt, and pepper. Bring to a boil, then reduce to a simmer. Cook for 30-40 minutes, until the lentils are tender.
3. Stir in the chopped spinach and cook for 2-3 minutes until wilted.
4. Add the lemon juice and stir to combine.
5. Serve the soup hot, with additional lemon wedges on the side if desired.

Baklava

Ingredients:

- 1 package phyllo dough (16 oz), thawed
- 2 cups mixed nuts (walnuts, pistachios, almonds), finely chopped
- 1 cup unsalted butter, melted
- 1 tsp ground cinnamon
- 1 cup granulated sugar
- 1 cup water
- 1/2 cup honey
- 1 tbsp lemon juice

Instructions:

1. Preheat the oven to 350°F (175°C).
2. Brush a 9x13-inch baking dish with melted butter. Layer 8 sheets of phyllo dough, brushing each sheet with butter.
3. Sprinkle a thin layer of chopped nuts and cinnamon over the phyllo. Repeat layering, buttering each sheet and adding more nuts until all the nuts are used, finishing with 8 more layers of phyllo dough.
4. Cut the assembled baklava into diamond or square shapes with a sharp knife.
5. Bake for 45-50 minutes, or until golden and crispy.
6. In a small saucepan, combine sugar, water, honey, and lemon juice. Bring to a boil, then reduce heat and simmer for 10 minutes.
7. Pour the syrup over the hot baklava as soon as it comes out of the oven. Let it cool completely before serving.

Stuffed Grape Leaves

Ingredients:

- 1 jar grape leaves, drained and rinsed
- 1 cup rice, rinsed
- 1/2 lb ground lamb or beef
- 1 onion, finely chopped
- 1/4 cup pine nuts (optional)
- 1/4 cup fresh dill, chopped
- 1/4 cup fresh parsley, chopped
- 1/4 cup olive oil
- 1 lemon, sliced
- 2 cups vegetable broth
- Salt and pepper to taste

Instructions:

1. In a large pan, heat olive oil over medium heat. Add the onion and cook until softened, about 5 minutes.
2. Add the ground meat, rice, pine nuts, dill, parsley, salt, and pepper. Stir to combine and cook for 5-7 minutes, until the meat is browned and the rice is slightly softened.
3. Place a grape leaf on a flat surface, stem side up. Add 1-2 tablespoons of the filling at the base of the leaf. Fold in the sides and roll it tightly into a cylinder. Repeat with the remaining leaves and filling.
4. Place the stuffed grape leaves seam-side down in a large pot. Layer the lemon slices on top and pour vegetable broth over the leaves.
5. Cover and simmer over low heat for 40-45 minutes until the rice is tender and the flavors have melded together.
6. Serve warm with a side of yogurt or lemon wedges.

Mediterranean Tuna Salad

Ingredients:

- 2 cans (5 oz) tuna in olive oil, drained
- 1/2 cup Kalamata olives, chopped
- 1/2 cup cherry tomatoes, halved
- 1/4 red onion, thinly sliced
- 1 cucumber, diced
- 1/4 cup fresh parsley, chopped
- 1/4 cup olive oil
- 2 tbsp lemon juice
- Salt and pepper to taste

Instructions:

1. In a large bowl, combine the tuna, olives, tomatoes, onion, cucumber, and parsley.
2. Drizzle with olive oil and lemon juice. Toss gently to combine.
3. Season with salt and pepper to taste.
4. Serve the salad chilled or at room temperature, with crusty bread or over a bed of greens.

Roasted Eggplant with Tahini Sauce

Ingredients:

- 2 large eggplants, sliced lengthwise
- 2 tbsp olive oil
- Salt and pepper to taste
- 1/4 cup tahini
- 2 tbsp lemon juice
- 1 clove garlic, minced
- 1 tbsp water (to thin sauce)
- Fresh parsley for garnish

Instructions:

1. Preheat the oven to 400°F (200°C). Line a baking sheet with parchment paper.
2. Brush eggplant slices with olive oil and season with salt and pepper. Arrange on the baking sheet.
3. Roast for 20-25 minutes until tender and golden brown.
4. While the eggplants roast, whisk together tahini, lemon juice, garlic, and water in a bowl until smooth.
5. Once the eggplant is cooked, drizzle with tahini sauce and garnish with fresh parsley.
6. Serve warm or at room temperature.

Seafood Paella

Ingredients:

- 1/4 cup olive oil
- 1 onion, chopped
- 2 cloves garlic, minced
- 1 bell pepper, chopped
- 2 tomatoes, chopped
- 1 1/2 cups Arborio rice or short-grain rice
- 1/4 tsp saffron threads
- 1/2 cup white wine
- 4 cups seafood or chicken broth
- 1 lb mixed seafood (shrimp, mussels, squid, etc.)
- 1/2 cup frozen peas
- Salt and pepper to taste
- Lemon wedges for garnish
- Fresh parsley for garnish

Instructions:

1. In a large paella pan or skillet, heat olive oil over medium heat. Add onion, garlic, and bell pepper, and sauté until softened.
2. Stir in tomatoes and cook for 5 minutes. Add rice and saffron, stirring to coat.
3. Pour in white wine and let it cook off. Add broth and bring to a simmer.
4. Add seafood and peas, and simmer for 15-20 minutes, until rice is tender and seafood is cooked through.
5. Season with salt and pepper to taste. Garnish with lemon wedges and parsley before serving.

Greek-Style Roast Lamb

Ingredients:

- 4 lbs leg of lamb
- 1/4 cup olive oil
- 4 cloves garlic, minced
- 2 tbsp dried oregano
- 1 tbsp fresh rosemary, chopped
- 1 lemon, juiced
- Salt and pepper to taste

Instructions:

1. Preheat oven to 375°F (190°C).
2. In a bowl, mix olive oil, garlic, oregano, rosemary, lemon juice, salt, and pepper to create a marinade.
3. Rub the marinade all over the lamb and let it marinate for at least 1 hour or overnight in the fridge.
4. Roast the lamb for 1.5 to 2 hours, or until it reaches your desired level of doneness. Let rest for 10 minutes before slicing.
5. Serve with roasted vegetables or a Greek salad.

Fennel and Orange Salad

Ingredients:

- 1 fennel bulb, thinly sliced
- 2 oranges, peeled and sliced
- 1/4 cup red onion, thinly sliced
- 2 tbsp olive oil
- 1 tbsp white wine vinegar
- Salt and pepper to taste
- Fresh dill for garnish

Instructions:

1. In a large bowl, combine fennel, orange slices, and red onion.
2. In a small bowl, whisk together olive oil, vinegar, salt, and pepper.
3. Drizzle the dressing over the salad and toss to combine.
4. Garnish with fresh dill and serve immediately.

Ratatouille

Ingredients:

- 2 tbsp olive oil
- 1 onion, chopped
- 1 bell pepper, chopped
- 2 zucchini, chopped
- 1 eggplant, chopped
- 4 tomatoes, chopped
- 2 cloves garlic, minced
- 1 tsp dried thyme
- 1 tsp dried basil
- Salt and pepper to taste
- Fresh basil for garnish

Instructions:

1. Heat olive oil in a large skillet over medium heat. Add onion, bell pepper, zucchini, and eggplant. Cook until softened, about 10 minutes.
2. Add tomatoes, garlic, thyme, basil, salt, and pepper. Simmer for 15-20 minutes, until the vegetables are tender.
3. Garnish with fresh basil and serve.

Grilled Eggplant with Feta Cheese

Ingredients:

- 2 eggplants, sliced
- 1/4 cup olive oil
- Salt and pepper to taste
- 1/2 cup crumbled feta cheese
- 1 tbsp fresh mint, chopped
- 1 tbsp balsamic glaze (optional)

Instructions:

1. Preheat the grill to medium-high heat.
2. Brush eggplant slices with olive oil and season with salt and pepper.
3. Grill for 3-4 minutes per side, until tender and charred.
4. Top with crumbled feta and fresh mint. Drizzle with balsamic glaze if desired.
5. Serve warm.

Lemon and Herb Roasted Potatoes

Ingredients:

- 2 lbs baby potatoes, halved
- 3 tbsp olive oil
- 1 lemon, zested and juiced
- 4 cloves garlic, minced
- 1 tsp dried oregano
- 1 tsp dried thyme
- Salt and pepper to taste
- Fresh parsley, chopped for garnish

Instructions:

1. Preheat the oven to 400°F (200°C).
2. In a large bowl, toss the halved potatoes with olive oil, lemon zest, lemon juice, garlic, oregano, thyme, salt, and pepper.
3. Spread the potatoes in a single layer on a baking sheet. Roast for 30-35 minutes, flipping halfway through, until golden and crispy.
4. Remove from the oven and garnish with fresh parsley before serving.

Octopus Salad

Ingredients:

- 1 lb octopus, cleaned and cut into pieces
- 2 tbsp olive oil
- 1/2 red onion, thinly sliced
- 1/2 cup cherry tomatoes, halved
- 1 cucumber, diced
- 1/4 cup Kalamata olives, chopped
- 1 tbsp fresh parsley, chopped
- 2 tbsp red wine vinegar
- 1 tbsp lemon juice
- Salt and pepper to taste

Instructions:

1. Bring a large pot of salted water to a boil. Add the octopus and cook for 40-45 minutes, or until tender. Drain and allow it to cool slightly.
2. Slice the octopus into bite-sized pieces.
3. In a large bowl, combine the octopus, onion, tomatoes, cucumber, olives, and parsley.
4. In a small bowl, whisk together the olive oil, red wine vinegar, lemon juice, salt, and pepper.
5. Pour the dressing over the salad and toss gently to combine. Serve chilled.

Mediterranean Chicken with Olives and Capers

Ingredients:

- 4 boneless, skinless chicken breasts
- 2 tbsp olive oil
- 1/2 cup Kalamata olives, pitted and chopped
- 2 tbsp capers, drained
- 1/2 cup chicken broth
- 1/4 cup white wine
- 1 tbsp fresh lemon juice
- 1 tsp dried oregano
- 2 cloves garlic, minced
- Salt and pepper to taste
- Fresh parsley, chopped for garnish

Instructions:

1. Season the chicken breasts with salt, pepper, and dried oregano.
2. Heat the olive oil in a large skillet over medium-high heat. Add the chicken breasts and cook for 6-7 minutes per side, until golden brown and cooked through. Remove the chicken from the skillet and set aside.
3. In the same skillet, add garlic and cook for 1 minute until fragrant. Add the olives, capers, chicken broth, white wine, and lemon juice. Stir well to combine.
4. Return the chicken to the skillet and simmer for 5-7 minutes, allowing the sauce to reduce slightly.
5. Serve the chicken with the olive and caper sauce, garnished with fresh parsley.

Tzatziki Sauce

Ingredients:

- 1 cup Greek yogurt
- 1 cucumber, grated and excess moisture squeezed out
- 2 cloves garlic, minced
- 1 tbsp fresh dill, chopped
- 1 tbsp olive oil
- 1 tbsp lemon juice
- Salt and pepper to taste

Instructions:

1. In a bowl, combine Greek yogurt, cucumber, garlic, dill, olive oil, and lemon juice.
2. Stir to combine and season with salt and pepper.
3. Chill in the refrigerator for at least 30 minutes before serving. Serve with grilled meats or as a dip.

Spinach and Feta Stuffed Chicken Breast

Ingredients:

- 4 boneless, skinless chicken breasts
- 1/2 cup feta cheese, crumbled
- 1 cup spinach, wilted and chopped
- 2 cloves garlic, minced
- 1 tbsp olive oil
- Salt and pepper to taste
- 1/2 cup breadcrumbs (optional)

Instructions:

1. Preheat oven to 375°F (190°C).
2. In a bowl, mix feta cheese, spinach, garlic, olive oil, salt, and pepper.
3. Cut a pocket into each chicken breast and stuff with the spinach and feta mixture.
4. Optional: Coat the chicken in breadcrumbs for a crispy exterior.
5. Heat olive oil in an ovenproof skillet over medium heat. Sear the chicken breasts for 3-4 minutes per side.
6. Transfer the skillet to the oven and bake for 20-25 minutes, until the chicken is fully cooked.

Orzo Salad with Tomatoes and Feta

Ingredients:

- 1 1/2 cups orzo pasta
- 1 pint cherry tomatoes, halved
- 1/2 cup feta cheese, crumbled
- 1/4 cup Kalamata olives, sliced
- 1/4 cup olive oil
- 1 tbsp red wine vinegar
- 1 tsp dried oregano
- Salt and pepper to taste

Instructions:

1. Cook the orzo according to package directions, then drain and let it cool.
2. In a large bowl, combine orzo, tomatoes, feta, olives, olive oil, vinegar, oregano, salt, and pepper.
3. Toss gently to combine and refrigerate for at least 30 minutes before serving.

Mediterranean Shrimp Scampi

Ingredients:

- 1 lb shrimp, peeled and deveined
- 3 tbsp olive oil
- 4 cloves garlic, minced
- 1/2 tsp red pepper flakes
- 1/4 cup white wine
- 2 tbsp lemon juice
- 1/4 cup fresh parsley, chopped
- Salt and pepper to taste

Instructions:

1. Heat olive oil in a large skillet over medium heat. Add garlic and red pepper flakes, and sauté for 1 minute.
2. Add shrimp and cook for 3-4 minutes, until pink and cooked through.
3. Stir in white wine and lemon juice, and cook for 2 more minutes.
4. Season with salt and pepper, and garnish with fresh parsley before serving.

Zaatar Roasted Chicken

Ingredients:

- 4 bone-in, skin-on chicken thighs
- 2 tbsp olive oil
- 2 tbsp zaatar spice blend
- 1 lemon, juiced
- 2 cloves garlic, minced
- Salt and pepper to taste

Instructions:

1. Preheat oven to 400°F (200°C).
2. In a small bowl, mix olive oil, zaatar, lemon juice, garlic, salt, and pepper.
3. Rub the spice mixture all over the chicken thighs.
4. Roast the chicken on a baking sheet for 35-40 minutes, until the chicken is golden brown and cooked through.

Saganaki (Fried Cheese)

Ingredients:

- 8 oz kefalotyri, kasseri, or halloumi cheese (cut into 1/2-inch thick slices)
- 1/4 cup flour
- 2 tbsp olive oil
- 1 tbsp lemon juice
- Fresh parsley for garnish

Instructions:

1. Heat olive oil in a large skillet over medium heat.
2. Dredge the cheese slices in flour and fry them for 2-3 minutes per side, until golden and crispy.
3. Drizzle with lemon juice and garnish with fresh parsley before serving.

Greek Meatballs with Yogurt Sauce

Ingredients:

- 1 lb ground beef or lamb
- 1/2 cup breadcrumbs
- 1/4 cup onion, finely chopped
- 2 cloves garlic, minced
- 1 tbsp fresh oregano, chopped
- 1 tsp ground cumin
- Salt and pepper to taste
- 1/2 cup Greek yogurt
- 1 tbsp lemon juice
- 1 tbsp fresh mint, chopped

Instructions:

1. Preheat oven to 375°F (190°C).
2. In a bowl, combine meat, breadcrumbs, onion, garlic, oregano, cumin, salt, and pepper. Form into meatballs.
3. Place meatballs on a baking sheet and bake for 20-25 minutes.
4. In a separate bowl, mix yogurt, lemon juice, and mint for the sauce.
5. Serve the meatballs with yogurt sauce.

Lemon and Garlic Marinated Olives

Ingredients:

- 1 1/2 cups mixed olives
- 2 tbsp olive oil
- 2 cloves garlic, sliced
- 1 tbsp lemon zest
- 1 tbsp lemon juice
- 1 tsp dried oregano
- Salt and pepper to taste

Instructions:

1. In a bowl, combine olives, olive oil, garlic, lemon zest, lemon juice, oregano, salt, and pepper.
2. Toss to coat, cover, and refrigerate for at least 1 hour before serving.

Mediterranean Veggie Pita Wraps

Ingredients:

- 4 pita breads
- 1 cup hummus
- 1 cucumber, sliced
- 1 tomato, sliced
- 1/4 red onion, thinly sliced
- 1/2 cup Kalamata olives, pitted and sliced
- 1/4 cup fresh parsley, chopped

Instructions:

1. Warm the pita breads slightly in the oven or on a skillet.
2. Spread a generous layer of hummus on each pita.
3. Add cucumber, tomato, onion, olives, and parsley.
4. Fold the pita over the filling and serve immediately.

Grilled Zucchini with Mint and Garlic

Ingredients:

- 4 zucchinis, sliced lengthwise
- 2 tbsp olive oil
- 2 cloves garlic, minced
- 1 tbsp fresh mint, chopped
- Salt and pepper to taste

Instructions:

1. Preheat the grill to medium-high heat.
2. Brush zucchini slices with olive oil and season with garlic, mint, salt, and pepper.
3. Grill the zucchini for 2-3 minutes per side, until tender and charred.
4. Serve warm.

Chickpea Stew with Spinach and Tomatoes

Ingredients:

- 2 cans (15 oz) chickpeas, drained and rinsed
- 1 tbsp olive oil
- 1 onion, chopped
- 2 cloves garlic, minced
- 1 can (14.5 oz) diced tomatoes
- 2 cups fresh spinach, chopped
- 1 tsp ground cumin
- 1/2 tsp paprika
- 1/4 tsp ground turmeric
- Salt and pepper to taste
- Fresh parsley for garnish

Instructions:

1. Heat olive oil in a large pot over medium heat. Add onion and garlic, sautéing until softened.
2. Add the diced tomatoes, cumin, paprika, turmeric, salt, and pepper. Stir well and cook for 5 minutes.
3. Add the chickpeas and spinach. Cook for another 5 minutes, until the spinach is wilted.
4. Garnish with fresh parsley before serving.

Roasted Red Pepper and Feta Dip

Ingredients:

- 2 red bell peppers, roasted and peeled
- 1 cup feta cheese, crumbled
- 2 tbsp olive oil
- 1 tbsp lemon juice
- 1 garlic clove, minced
- Salt and pepper to taste
- Fresh parsley for garnish

Instructions:

1. Place the roasted red peppers, feta, olive oil, lemon juice, garlic, salt, and pepper into a blender or food processor.
2. Blend until smooth and creamy.
3. Transfer to a bowl and garnish with fresh parsley. Serve with pita chips or fresh vegetables.

Grilled Lamb Chops with Garlic and Rosemary

Ingredients:

- 8 lamb chops
- 3 cloves garlic, minced
- 2 tbsp fresh rosemary, chopped
- 2 tbsp olive oil
- 1 tbsp lemon juice
- Salt and pepper to taste

Instructions:

1. In a small bowl, combine garlic, rosemary, olive oil, lemon juice, salt, and pepper.
2. Rub the mixture over the lamb chops and let them marinate for at least 30 minutes.
3. Preheat the grill to medium-high heat. Grill the lamb chops for 4-5 minutes per side, until cooked to your desired level of doneness.
4. Serve immediately.

Couscous-Stuffed Bell Peppers

Ingredients:

- 4 bell peppers, tops cut off and seeds removed
- 1 cup couscous
- 1 1/4 cups vegetable broth
- 1/2 cup feta cheese, crumbled
- 1/4 cup Kalamata olives, chopped
- 1/4 cup fresh parsley, chopped
- 1 tbsp olive oil
- Salt and pepper to taste

Instructions:

1. Preheat oven to 375°F (190°C).
2. In a small pot, bring vegetable broth to a boil. Stir in couscous, cover, and remove from heat. Let sit for 5 minutes.
3. Fluff the couscous with a fork and stir in feta, olives, parsley, olive oil, salt, and pepper.
4. Stuff the bell peppers with the couscous mixture and place in a baking dish.
5. Cover with foil and bake for 25-30 minutes. Remove foil and bake for an additional 5 minutes to slightly brown the tops.

Greek-Style Braised Okra

Ingredients:

- 1 lb fresh okra, trimmed
- 1 can (14.5 oz) diced tomatoes
- 1 onion, chopped
- 3 cloves garlic, minced
- 1/2 cup olive oil
- 1 tsp dried oregano
- Salt and pepper to taste

Instructions:

1. Heat olive oil in a large pan over medium heat. Add onion and garlic, and sauté until softened.
2. Add the okra, diced tomatoes, oregano, salt, and pepper. Stir well.
3. Cover and simmer on low heat for 30-40 minutes, stirring occasionally, until the okra is tender.
4. Serve warm with a drizzle of olive oil.

Lemon and Herb Grilled Sea Bass

Ingredients:

- 4 sea bass fillets
- 2 tbsp olive oil
- 1 lemon, zest and juice
- 1 tbsp fresh thyme, chopped
- 1 tbsp fresh parsley, chopped
- Salt and pepper to taste

Instructions:

1. In a bowl, mix olive oil, lemon juice, lemon zest, thyme, parsley, salt, and pepper.
2. Brush the sea bass fillets with the mixture and let them marinate for 15-20 minutes.
3. Preheat the grill to medium-high heat. Grill the fish for 3-4 minutes per side, until cooked through.
4. Serve with lemon wedges.

Pita Bread with Olive Oil and Herbs

Ingredients:

- 4 pita breads
- 1/4 cup olive oil
- 1 tbsp fresh thyme, chopped
- 1 tbsp fresh rosemary, chopped
- 1 garlic clove, minced
- Salt to taste

Instructions:

1. Preheat oven to 375°F (190°C).
2. Brush pita bread with olive oil, and sprinkle with thyme, rosemary, garlic, and salt.
3. Place pita on a baking sheet and bake for 8-10 minutes, until crisp and golden.
4. Slice into wedges and serve as an appetizer or side dish.

www.ingramcontent.com/pod-product-compliance
Lightning Source LLC
LaVergne TN
LVHW081342060526
838201LV00055B/2795